Additional praise for Peculia

In her debut full-length collection, DeMi
the *Peculiar Heritage* of African American women. She pays homage
to historical ancestors like Tituba, Harriet Tubman, and Josephine
Baker; her own mother plaiting her hair in "a lineage of designs;" and
literary influences ranging from Emily Dickinson to Toni Morrison,
Phil Levine to Claudia Rankine, as well as Langston Hughes.

—Grace Bauer,
author of *Unholy Heart: New and Selected Poems*

DeMisty D. Bellinger writes powerful, intelligent, and lyrical poems.
In one section she imagines herself an enslaved person who escapes
northward. She successfully writes political poems that are well crafted,
moving, and elegant.

—Marge Piercy, author of 17 novels, including
the *New York Times* bestseller *Gone to Soldiers*

By setting historical trauma against various natural backdrops,
including a stunning sequence of poems for each phase of the moon,
Bellinger unveils how rooted these atrocities are in the physical world.
Here is a poet of skillful ambition and wisdom who demonstrates again
and again, through deep political and personal study, that poetry can
be the purest form of protest.

—Marianne Kunkel,
author of *Hillary, Made Up*

PECULIAR HERITAGE

-POEMS-

DeMISTY D. BELLINGER

Mason Jar Press | Baltimore, MD

Published by
Mason Jar Press
Baltimore, MD

Printed by Spencer Printing in Honesdale, PA.

Learn more about Mason Jar Press at masonjarpress.com.

Dedicated to
Natasha "Peaches" Sims
and Helen Lampkins.
I miss you both!

A History

PECULIAR HERITAGE

PART I

"When I found I had crossed that line, I looked at my hands to see if I was the same person. There was such a glory over everything; the sun came like gold through trees, and over the fields, and I felt like I was in Heaven."

—Harriet Tubman

"When my oldest brother hear us is free he give a whoop, run and jump a high fence, and told mammy goodbye. Den he grab me up and hug and kiss me and say, 'Brother gone, don't 'spect you ever see me no more.'"

—Susan Ross, born in Magnolia Springs, Texas, circa 1862, enslaved by Cheater Horn

A Peculiar Heritage

I.
if you look at her eyes
straight on after you've
taken from her every
one that she's thought to
love and if you see the
whites glisten and the browns
grow big and she appears
plaintive, she appears hurt but
not depleted, do remember that
heifers and sows and ewes too,
would give such eyes but soon
resolve, like the Negress,
to forget.

You could just not look at her eyes.

II.
if you look at her eyes and forget
the other livestock on your farm,
does it make it easier to take her
where your wife won't see?

if you see her as livestock,
would that make it harder to
take her?

if she is nothing more than a
dam, then what she dams also
comes from you. what is it
that comes from you?

Tituba

I'll tell you what you want me to if I can be free
It is cold here, and I don't know the old England—
This is all new to me.

I'll tell you what you want me to if I can be free
I would traverse this coast on foot, float down
The Atlantic to warmer waters.

I'll tell you anything. Yes, say 'witch.' Yes, say 'spell.'
I don't care for tea or the way you speak, the
Way you don't sing.

I close my eyes, I'll cast a spell for me and say aloud: Yes
I see waters the color of the stones found on the shores
And palm fronds waving.   .   .

I don't hurt the children, I say. I say, "I do not hurt them."
I say the devil came, I say anything, I say it because I think
They'll uncage me.

I say anything. I tell them stories of animals with the minds of men
Stories of dances and cats bidding the devil's doing if
They'll have me no more.

I tell them because I want to be free, if they want me
No more with the family, no more in Salem, no more coldness
I'll tell them a story.

There Was Such a Glory:
An Ode to Harriet Tubman

I: There Was Such a Glory

Over everything, the world look gold-gilded
    these Northern trees with their shimmering leaves
    this river full of mud running loudly in praise
    my fingers and fingernails, though scruffed and
        scratched and filled with dirt
    the grasses growing glowed when the wind blew
    these field flowers that I did not know (I knelt and smelt
        them; I shuddered but did not sob)

It was the sun that shone, sure, but it was that I could see how
    the sun shone, what the light hit and what hid from it
    I could feel warm, and a breeze, and concentrate on that
    I could not look over my shoulder and, my Lord, I could
    sit on the grass, for a minute, for minutes, and longer.

II: Because of Kessiah

Overheard on a network as strong as
gale winds blow across city, prairie, and
forests, riding river waves from the South to
the North, news from a never-wanted home.

Trade for comfort and unfettered life because
of Kessiah, because of love, because
a freedom as wide as this should
be shared with her and her family.

And back where glory reigns, rest
only as long as it takes to catch a breath,
because freedom is sweet as summer's
rain and cannot be hoarded, because

of indiscriminate love, go down
over and over again. "You'll be
free or die," to those too afraid to
continue, soon they go: upward, forward.

And when the men who make the rules
clash over morality and slavery, revolt
against those who call themselves rebels.
There is liberty, or there is death.

III: Nurse Cook Spy

On the deck of the gunboat,
did she wear a dress such as
those women wore in that
era? I imagine she wore boots
blacker than her skin, but
just as well-worn and ready
to carry her. Did she smile as
the iron-clad boat traversed
waters deceivingly calm? Did
the men look to her as a leader?
Did she look at them as her men?
Was she, before going into battle
and freeing even more,
a nurse to the Union soldiers?
their cook? Was she, even then,
spying?

Gingerly

A pungent plant—
      Gnarly root
      Pulled before purply flowers
      Populate the head of a vine
      Creeping up from underground
      papery skin lighter than my own,
      And the flesh inside office supply color.

A versatile plant—
      bite as sharp as pepper
      almost unpleasant, a taste acquired
      a coveted spice
      this root too sharp for
      caution. Too hot for
      care.

Call for Escape Abecedarian

About
Baby
Closing her eyes tight against the
Darkness, I offer this:
Escape only if it's for survival.
Freedom comes to those who don't want it too.
Go toward the wind the when it is quiet, don't just
Hear, Baby Girl, but listen.
Indigo is only a good color when
Joy is in the air.
Killing is only murder when
Life is worthwhile.
Moan, but only under your breath,
Neglect your aches, your toes that itch.
Open your eyes when you feel unsafe and
Pray when you can pick a god
Quiet enough for you.
Resistance is an art practiced over a lifetime and
Strengthened in use, like any muscle.
Tenaciously hold onto what it will mean to walk
Under a clear sky, bright moon, on
Verdant grass covered in dusk-time dew.
Work your way north, and north again, past
Xeric grasses and fir trees, past
Yonder hate and
Zealous desire of your body.

Neo-Escape Chant

Her curtain caught on something old when she ran with it down the street screaming for some man called Peter or Paul I can't remember which but I saw her get caught on something rusty—the curtain—and jagged and her left leg raised in flight "Peter!" or was it "Paul!"? her lips drawn back in ways that writers say that a character's lips are drawn back in what looks like a grimace but if I pictured her here: look—a smile? A long 'A' sound or maybe a long 'E'? her left leg raised with knee bent as if to step down and as if to go further her right leg behind her like running but she's caught with her curtain holding her back and keeping her here with the rest of us, that curtain curled around a jagged, rusty, ancient thing that looks like tetanus.

LUNAR JOURNEY

The Woman Was Leaving

The woman was leaving—
    Or staying
        I was the one leaving
            And after four miles, I will meet someone
A man maybe, and his wife
    The man is called Abel
        The wife is called Missus Abel and is sure to be there
The man will be white and wearing a large, woolen hat,
black as the night
    I'd miss save for the light leaking from the moon
        He will ask, "Are ye lost?"
        I will say, "Sir, I believe I am."
            Missus Abel will say, "I know the way."
Missus Abel will walk north and east,
    Abel will follow her,
        I will bring up the end.
        And when all is safe,
I will walk in the middle.

New Moon

There is no moon.
No houses with lights on
and clouds cover the sky—
I close my eyes and there is no change
but what I imagine are my fingernails
pink against the darkness of my hands
nails broken in places,
skin puckered with oversaturation.

Tonight,
it is cold.
I learn quickly what shivering is.
My teeth chatter like
the spoons a man used for music,
whose name I never learned—
I heard him called uncle and Joe and boy,
but none of those seemed quite right—
he had two spoons the Woman gave to him
because they were ruined.
I think she just wanted to hear him play
just wanted to rest on her cotton-covered arm
tatted cuffs, and
smile at him.

I feel snow
and I know it's snow because it's too thick to
be rain
and my teeth make the sound
of the spoons dancing across the man's knuckles
I count in fives
I know one five and two fives
I walk five steps and five more—

I walk until I've exhausted the numbers I know and hear,
"stop."

I hold out my hands ahead of me
feeling only the wind blow between the webs
of my fingers
and the snow melting instantly on my skin,
I close my eyes: I see
the precarious pink of my fingernails
I say:
"I'm sure I'm lost."

Waxing Crescent

These are things I'm sure of:

My eyes, which I imagine are brown, are now all white.
My skin will stay scarred. Blood from barbed plants will always line
    my legs.
My stomach will forever rumble like low clouds, like rain
    somewhere west of me.
My stomach will forever feel the weight it carried for months
    and months again.
My thighs will ache, my hips will ache, my back will ache,
    my feet—god, my feet.
My mind would wander, question freedom and its worth.
    (the weight of—)
My desire for the moon to grow completely full and white
    and happy, round as
Mister and Missus Robinson's oldest son who took after no one.

The woman who stood next to me, pulled me back a little
The woman was as white as the moon, as the night that fell around us
—I dodged lest the sky hit me
The woman said, with her hat on, crowning her face
In a way that I understood to both expose and hide her beauty

She said, "You'll have to forgive them."
I said, "I don't know that word."

First Quarter

The moon tonight, two sides of one.
I stare at the white side
And let my eyes blur in tears until
It grows fatter than it is:
The pale pools over between the stars.
I close my eyes and see a full moon:
Round as forgiveness.
I cringe at benevolence towards those I've quit,
Enough so to make me open my eyes.

On the other side, there is an absence of whiteness.
The shadowed half of the moon extends silently across the sky
Offering a muted possibility of not even forgetting.
I lifted up into that darkness and, unflinching,
I go where I am welcome to entertain
The freedom to hate.

Waxing Gibbous

When the moon was too bright, we stayed in a little shed on someone's farm. There was one window and it was broken. The glass was almost softened in the edges where space was made. The glass, that had undoubtedly fallen whenever it was cracked, had been swept up. It was easy to imagine little sharp shards, sheets of brokenness shattered further by work shoes, glass ground into shimmery bits, glass catching moonlight like crystals and expense, like sand again. I brush the toe of my boot against the floor, listen to the dirt slide like scouring soap against wood. I peek out the window and see the moon, its light as white as dried cow dung, its shape wobbling to fullness, and I imagine days I'll spend here in this little shed.

Nights Spent Flying (New Moon Reprise)

I've lost count of the days that I close my eyes against,
try to sleep in spite of the sunlight seeping through,
red globules dance across my sight

and this day is cooler than any days I've known.

I lay on a quilt I made with a woman called Rebecca, a woman
called Ruth,
and a woman we called ma'am because even though she was just
like us, she stood tall—
like us, she sewed for relaxation and knew enough to laugh at doing
work for pleasure.

I close my eyes tighter and I can see their smiles, their high cheekbones.

The fat quarters were already worn bare and soft as brushed fresh
cotton
when we got them, and the stuffing was only more scraps,
so the quilt was thin, and beneath it I felt the prick of the grass tips,
the digs of the gravel,

the grass and mud, cooling towards autumn.

Still, I was heading away and even in the light of day,
where I tried to sleep hiding beneath the trees of a hidden stand—
I slept. I was learning to feel good. Heading away to a life of dreams

following a star like mythical wise men.

Full Moon

Her face
eats the light

the light
illuminates her skin

her skin
pocked by disease

and age lines
each contour three

four times.

I see in her
capability of hate

I stop breathing long enough
to understand the sounds of night—

I've heard these noises
all my life

but tonight
I get to listen.

Birds that are silent when the sun shines

Bugs whose wings whisk the night air

Wild dogs baying at the same moon
I cower under.

Carefully, I breathe again and hear the noise
I make join the nocturnal ensemble.

I hear, too, her breathing beneath me
wonder what she'd think if

she'd wake up.

If she wakes now,
she will see me hovering

over her, she would hear the animals,
the wind forcing the leaves and the

grass to drum like rainfall. If she wakes
up, she would be disoriented

and here I know I should move away
but I can't stop marveling over

her face and the light collected there
from the moon. I want to wake

to thank her, but I let her sleep.

Hers is the of face of hurt,
but she is not that, I know.

Like the moon, I watch her;
she guides me.

Waning Gibbous

Looks like a face turning
slightly away from
me as I'm still looking—
        still trying to figure out
if this is friend or if
this is foe or if
this is nobody at all to

be concerned with
and I can reach out
my arm, my
hand, to touch her elbow—
just the inner part where the
skin is often described as
soft as tissue paper but I
know the skin there is
softer than that, I know
the skin there is as
secret
as words not even whispered,
words only breathed
in the darkest of nights under
a sky full of stars
to nobody at all.

Looks like a lie
that was told to me
when I was on the edge
of dreaming, when I was
young, when I was in
the arms of someone I love
and trusted, but accepted

the lie, and learned while
eyes flutter against the
weight of sleep—
the difference between a lie
and fib   and story.

Those who lie, I learn
may love me;
those who fib, I learn
are trying to trick me
and those who tell stories

are nobody—
nobody at all.

Last Quarter

The taste of
communion bread—broken
by soft hands, jagged
half pressing against
my tongue—melts in
the skies above me
Tells me:
Half is here.

The moon lights the field
We don't even hide in
We lay silently on our backs
Eating stale bread.

Wet grass smell
And the dew that covers it
go to sleep, she tells me.
Tomorrow, we're almost home.

Waning Crescent

Tomorrow morning, I'll be done.

It's cold this evening, I'm told, but I'm sweating.

I am not a lazy woman; I will find work.

Everyone sleeps, I wander. I've walked for miles, and still wander.

Everyone is at ease now, but I look over my shoulder.

Up above me, a crescent moon, and I wonder if it's far enough—

Tomorrow morning, my walk will be short.

I'll rest, but I'm sure that I'll always wander.

I'll say free, but I'll keep looking

Over my shoulder.

June 19, 1865

emancipation has too many syllables and I don't have the words for syllables yet / I haven't the experience to understand what it could possibly mean and would be for me / major general has too many titles and none of them are master / he says free and some of us laugh / I step gingerly forward and nothing / for two years major general granger says, we been free / and I take another step forward and I hear / nothing / I walk on and I don't even hear / a dog / I'm still walking

PART II

"It all proceeds from the same deep logic. It's the same logic that sold lives for profit in the Atlantic slave trade, it's the logic that gives us sweatshops and oil spills, and it's the logic that is right now pushing us headlong toward ecological collapse and climate change."

—Jason Hickel and Martin Kirk

"The proletarians have nothing to lose but their chains. They have a world to win."

—Karl Marx

"I thank you for your question, but I'm sorry to say we're capitalists."

—Nancy Pelosi

Neo-blues Song

What keeps me awake at night
lulls you to sleep at ten.

There are ten bars more,
but I can't sleep.

There is a key change,
but I won't hear it.

I can't keep up with the tempo,
I have forgotten all the words.

Things are changing too fast for me,
shifting when I'm sitting.

I'd get up, but I'm so down.
That's how the blues go: I'm so down.

Who knows what repeats—
what keeps me away at night,

Lulls you, lullabies you.

1925

I
Start the diagram
of the Negro
from the nose.
Point to the left nostril
with horizontal line,
type in Copperplate Gothic
"outsized."
Somehow, in the illustration,
radiate out from the nipples (
make them huge, the areolas,
and make the nipples daggers
) somehow, show the kink of
the hair spire like black wires,
somehow, make it smile.
Point to the hair with horizontal
line, type: Coarse.

II
Nigger toes: Brazil nuts
Nigger lips: wetting the butt of a shared cigarette
Nigger rich: pay day, or the first of the month

III
        from the shoulders.
Show that the shoulders are broad.
Show them in relationship to the head:
Head is small, make the mouth
smile (and look mean and look animalistic and look dumb
and pout and leer and
) the whites of the eyes
the white teeth

should be all white: an
absence of color like the skin—
make that, too, an absence of color but:
negative/positive
teeth should not gnash as much
as flash out at

IV

Her feet grew more even though she was done growing. It was the babies. They made them large and when pressed fully on the ground, splayed out like beasts apart from her. Her toes gnarled into something seemingly unhuman. Place her left foot on a sheet of white paper and trace it and find the pencil jerks around the unnatural lines formed by bunions and scars

Inside Zelli's at Night between the Wars[*]

"The nigger drummer waved"
> —and I swayed how what I imagined palm trees to sway
> —ignored the gay Parisians around me, their white faces lit
> > by candles on tables, by gas lights
> —like palm trees: I held my arms up—
> —you could see my black fingers moving the physical air
> > working the winds around me

"Damn good drummer"
> —I rattled my knees, brought my hands down and placed
> them there
> > like Josephine, I bowed my legs and wobbled them back
> > and forth
> —I felt the rhythm, the common time of it, the heartbeat of
> it, and I
> —danced as surely my ancestors in Africa—
> —closed my eyes and felt the heat of the continent

"The drummer shouted"
> —my eyes opened up so I could see what—

"the drummer chanted. Then turned to his sticks."
> —I chanted back
> —sensed the Parisians' eyes on my bared back
> —I shimmied so that my beaded hem bucked and clattered:
> > an accompanying rhythm, my legs their own sticks, his
> > sticks an extension,
> > his sticks actual tree trunks
> > his sticks Congo worthy

....

[*] All quotes are from *The Sun Also Rises* by Ernest Hemingway.

"the drummer sang softly."

  —I stopped dancing. his voice hushed in the timbre of his drum, in the volume of the band, in Montmartre, in the waters across the Mediterranean, washed to Algeria, traveling down to Côte d'Ivoire, from here: the drummer sang softly, dulce, inaudibly.

Big Men and the North

This is work. This is a sacrifice to the moneyed. This is a goat gotten from a farm that people cannot believe exists in the western part of this state. Look: the farm lies just beyond those mountains.

These are two men with shiny, patent leather shoes that they shopped for. Those men: they chose those shoes during an hour or half an hour on a busy day and they tried them on, looked in the mirror that came up to their knees, saw how their tailored hems fell over the tongue of the shoe. They fantasized walking to somewhere great with these shoes on, they dreamt of big things happening because of those shoes.

This is what work is: slitting throats of farm goats and collecting the offal in a bin. This is the messiness of assimilating: big men becoming great men.

Life Death, Knows Doesn't Know
—after Bruce Nauman

Life's like that sometimes
I know how you feel
They don't
     She doesn't
     She has a freedom
     that's not available
     to us
Life's like that
Know as we move toward
  the end
 that nothing matters
 Death don't care
 We move toward pleasure
 & away from pain
 Life, death
Both know, & doesn't know

Portrait of Lady of a Certain Age

I'm in a department store in the women's accessory section. Elevator music is playing, though I don't think I've ever heard elevator music in a department store (or in an elevator) or anywhere and I'm looking at pairs of pantyhose, or tights, or Lycra or Spandex, and nothing is quite my size. Almost my size—too small or too large. I take folds of Nylon or Lycra or Spandex between my index finger and the tall finger and run my fingers along the smooth, tiny bumps. They won't fit.

Someone is feeding me something sweet and they ask, "Do you taste the honey?" And I'll answer, "Yes, yes, I taste the honey." "Do you taste the brown sugar? It's rich. It's organic." And I'll say, "Yes, I do taste the brown sugar." "And do you taste the vanilla?" "Yes, I do taste it. I taste the vanilla."

My hair itches, but I won't scratch. I hit my head swiftly with my flattened hand to disturb the scalp—the closest I'll come to scratching. I either cannot mess my hair up because I'm going somewhere or because I am getting a relaxer.

I am breathing both silently and heavily. I am crying into my pillow. I shake lightly. I don't want to disturb the person I am in bed with. I am not married. I do not know if there is someone in bed with me. I cry more because I do not want to die alone.

I wake up. I go to the department store and circulate through the men's accessory section. I say to a clerk, "I want to buy a wallet, but I don't want it to be leather."

A Collective Resistance

That we whirl in spite of defiantly
standing still, and we move through crowds with a
hardwired wherewithal so physical
contact is rare and, when it occurs, brief.

      We from above ook singular: one.
A colony weaving between grids for
purpose. For reasons. For the greater good.
In earth tones and black to blend: collective.

That one woman who now climbs up the stairs
of a building higher than fog seems different,
but she's only more of us. We follow
suit. That we climb up stairs and push buttons.

That we remain stagnant even though we revolve,
is lost on us. That surpasses us. Moves us.

Windsor Knot

Remember the scene in Gatsby / Daisy sailing shirts through the roomspace / I felt stuffy reading that novel when placed in / Gatsby's long islanded mansion / Imagine instead: waters outside / Calm ripples / Ties denoting masculinity / Colors and patterns denoting what is manmade / Rigidity of Western men / Dampened, wetted, dowsed / Imagine instead: a baptism in money / Capitalism mistaken for love / Economy of care / A wealth of undrinkable water / A sea of tightened ties.

and Then

And then she gets off the bus. Negotiating those heels,
She almost trips on her way off the lowering platform,
Almost hears someone try to save her, which was too much

For her to consider. Then she walks toward her house,
On the corner she hesitates, not sure if she had to stop
At the store or if she has everything she needs at home.

The thought there was so much in her apartment: Every
Thing she ever needed in the world in her drawers,
Her refrigerator, the cabinets, between the cracks
where she couldn't sweep.

Now, the light blinks the walking pictogram.
She doesn't move. Everything at home she'd ever need.
In her home, enough to cause her to pause.
              These heels contain me, she thought, then:
              These hills around her, around everyone, and then—

The Black Woman Talks about Lakes

Lake Michigan is the first to come to mind,
        If you want to talk about lakes.
The lakes I know are here in America;
I've only heard of lakes in Europe;
I can't afford to see the lakes in Africa.
Nothing's new. And nothing is old.

The lake I love, Michigan, I know has been segregated
In Milwaukee and Chicago
It's so wide, I can't see across it.
It's so deep, I can't touch bottom.
It's so tainted and coveted—waters that are supposed to
Run clear
Give the poor
Lead and cryptosporidium.

I know lakes private
And wooded and hidden.

I've grown to miss Lake Michigan
And hate it.

Sowing Season

My mother's fingers
th-rip th-rip th-rip
through my coarse hair
one over two over three—
      one over two over three
thousands of ringed circlets
circling each other
      (th-rip th-rip th-rip)
thousands of times
braiding histories of the women
      before her
      into my hair

My mother parts furrows
onto the scalp beneath
the mound of my wooly hair
scratching
      (scree shee scree),
         charting
rows of roads crossed
by the women before her
      into my hair

My mother's fingers recall
lineage of designs
cross continents, cross ideas
crossing corn rows
      th-rip th-rip th-rip
      plaiting Africa
      into my hair

PART III

"Resistance is the secret of joy."

—Alice Walker

Real Estate Mogul

I will destroy everything you've created
and build instead something paler,
freckle-speckled, gold-gilded
tell the people it's as good as my name
See the egress!

War Chant

Tell us about
America
when it was palatable.

Sing to us
in perfect bass
vibrato quaking
the ground beneath.

Plait our hair in
perfect well-
greased rows and
rubber-banded ends!

Oh, tell us about
the America
we now fight for.

PROTEST POEMS

I. (Protest Poems)

I keep writing protest poems in comfort:
near middle-class behind a desktop computer
in notebooks full of unlined, acid-free paper
in my mind on the way to work, from work

At work, in classes, I prompt my students to write
and I write along with them: protest poems.
　　Words are witty signage and pink on brown cardboard
lines marching from margin to margin,
I imagine me shouting, but silently—

(in comfort), safely, resisting what's coming
pushing back, protesting it. In poetry,
I'm a protestant in democracy
I berate my representatives, I move
mountains and streets. I stop traffic

with verse and rhymes and slant rhymes and no rhymes
I won't be moved from my office chair
I write letters I won't send save for publishers
of little magazines and I'll sit, sending out.

The arguments I have are rhythmic
my stances stand
in song without music
without sound
without

II. (Peaceful)

What would we be
had Christ pulled himself
from the cross & knocked
that hateful structure down?
Would he be Christ?
Would we stand for persecution?

What would we be if
Jesus did not ask his
Father, but used his strength? What if he
saved himself? Could
we be saved?

What if Gandhi found
an elephant gun? What
if he pointed it at
Britain & said, "the
sun will set here?"
Who would King have
looked to?

And what if King
got sick of spite
& spittle & the word
nigger thrown like
spears?

Would that have mattered?

III. (Ontology of)

hand-lettered signs with witty words
colors bright, colors bland and black,
letters in big, block capitals,
exclamation points are used
thought, goes into where the hands will hold the board, or
if not poster board, then carefully carved cardboard boxes
where the ink in the markers make a sound like a stick against a
guiro
and the smell from the ink stinks of dangerous chemicals
and the angry tears are wiped by the heel of blued and blackened
and reddened hands
the colors smear on your face
you consider comfortable shoes and debate on
wearing a Fitbit, wonder if you should bring an energy bar
you charge your phone and you pack gum and wonder if you
should make a playlist
fill your water bottle
you'll stay all day
you'll be there all night
you'll camp out
stay a lifetime
and worry if—
each step you take in those walking shoes
     holding the sign until your wrists ache
     yelling slogans til your throat is scratchy
—this is enough?

IV. (Reprise)

What bothers me are the cigarette butts underfoot
What bothers me is the woman behind me who
won't answer her child I can't see,
I can't be seen, I say something here,
I can't be heard. I say something at all,
I won't be heard. What bothers me is
that we keep stopping. Before me: shoulders
& backs, one tall guy's ass. I don't know
why we're stopping. I'm losing the chant,
I catch it, I chant, I try to be heard.
It starts to rain & someone starts singing,
Her voice like a call to love and a call to arms.
I grab my friend and move toward the left,
We get out of the crowd.
I want to say that this is not quite what I want
But I can't be heard.

PART III

-CONTINUED-

Morning Pledge

If at morning assembly,
we read a poem vetted by learned aficionados
instead of pledging our lives to a symbol,
then we could delve into symbolism.

How can we feel martial while contemplating
burying children at home,
wide hips, and supermarkets?

Or maybe this is the stuff that makes
us rise to war, to protect the sanctity of
running Mexicans and tender buttons.

Here: take your hand from your heart
and kneel as in prayer, read with me
about dried-out raisins and
deferred dreams.

Love during Unrest

You lean towards me and
I'll lean towards you.

You pass by me: go over;
I'll pass by you.

You're slick by me
I'm rough like clotted oils
Tarnished patina
I imagine grasping on:
Little nappy hairs at the nape of your neck
Little curls clinging on—

You're lean like arrows moving towards or away
I'm leaning like Eros, but bent away.

You lean towards me and
I'll lean towards you.

Pussy Willow

This common shrubbery's male form has a "wooly catkin." A catkin is the "flowering spike" "typically downy, pendulous." You prefer fuzzy to wooly but sure, wooly. Catkin roots are Dutch and mean something like kitten. Wooly or fuzzy downy pendulous kitten. You know this plant. You see silk flowers or dried flowers or just the male form of this plant in a tall vase, and the plant is erect and pointing ever upward. You take your index finger and thumb of your left hand and absently stroke one of the little white wooly bulbs when talking to someone about anything else but catkin and fuzzy or wooly or kittens and you close your eyes briefly, shudder slightly, feeling a little mischievous as the hairs of this plant tickle the pads of your fingers, and you're still talking about politics or anything else and you grab this maleness of this shrubbery and feel some level of control.

Nasty Girls Pantoum

"Do you think I'm a nasty girl?" Vanity 6
"The only nasty thing I like is the nasty groove." Miss Jackson

Am I such a nasty woman?
I've cleaned my hair, I've clipped my nails,
I have made sure to smile and, baby,
I'm not being so mean.

I've cleaned my hair, I've clipped my nails
I washed each inch of my body
So I wouldn't be so mean
And dressed in well-laundered clothes.

I washed each inch of my body
And didn't linger on the special parts
Got dressed in well-laundered clothes
Left the house with good intentions

I didn't linger on the special parts
So I wouldn't hurt anyone's feelings
I went high, I stay high
When the rest of the world went low.

So I wouldn't hurt anyone's feelings,
I acted like a perfect lady
When the rest of the world went low.
Am I such a nasty woman?

A Genesis

Had the nerve
to speak her mind
translate what transpired to
words warped by years of
distress and apprehension
the audacity to clear her throat
and purse her lips until everyone saw
them spew a truth grubby with righteousness,
paltry pleading,
wretched words:
such a nasty woman.

Orlando

"Sometimes I feel like throwing my hands up in the air"

—Florence + the Machine

"Oh, make me wanna holler/ And throw up both my hands"

—Marvin Gaye

I want the biggest party
I want every DJ ever to make a playlist
I want sparkly makeup and glow sticks,
Whistles and noisemakers
I want to have to yell over the music
I want to stop dancing but I don't want to stop dancing
I want to feel the floor bounce beneath me
I want driving bass lines paving the way
I want everything colored rainbow, rainbow, rainbow
I want salsa music and merengue and samba
I want it to be so humid and sweaty and hot that my hair sticks to
      my face,
To your face, others' faces covered in glitter
I want to see teeth glowing in the black light
I want to be sprayed with water
I want tropical drinks
I want breaks in the music where I can catch secrets screamed over
      non-noise
Then I want the music to come in louder than before
I want to holler woo, throw up both my hands
I want happiness to be tactile, kinetic, joining us like scales on fish
I want men kissing men and men kissing men and men kissing men
I want women kissing women and women kissing women
I want to kiss everyone
I want the biggest party and to see everybody dance now

In June
When it's already hot
Where the sunrises are the color of Elizabeth Bishop's dreams
I want the sun to always rise
I want to know there will be a tomorrow

Ways to Escape

Those of us who can't pray can still want. Today I
want, and my teeth are on end, so when I
shudder, they click. I can bow my head, I can
close my eyes, I can give silence. I
want so much my throat goes dry and my
left eye twitches. On loop, I sing the
rhyme about making a dollar from fifteen
cents because ends don't quite meet and
that sets my teeth to chattering and I get
tired of wanting.

Those of us who can't pray can still wish.
I'll look up and find the brightest star or satellite,
wish without restraint for what I need. I'll
raise my hands to the skies and wait for
fulfillment until my neck feels strained, my
elbows ache from straightening, my shoulders
grow sore. Here, I hear if wishes were fishes
and the world goes sour.

Those of us who can't pray can still hope, can still
dream. These words are the same things here; both
strive towards a greater good, something we deem
obtainable. Hope is only as powerful as the others—
all are strong as prayer to the unfaithful
and the uninitiated. Pray for only what you need.
Be careful, I know, for what you wish for.
The word pray peters into
something horrid.

Brutal

I: It Was Brutal[†]

We see how tragic that life was
      with distance and time,
            the clearest vision,
and then it's too late.

But we can ask with something
      like true curiosity and concern
          if any life is untragic
if anything can be just in time.

     Or we can ask,
          with something like
     desperate dignity
if any life is worthy of tragedy—

shouldn't something as glorious as
      dying in multicolored plumes
          and staccatoed, even rhythms
be reserved for the revered?

Of course, we can emphatically
      bow our heads in
          reverence, with something like empathy,
lids lowered against the glare.

. . . .

[†] Barack Obama when speaking to family members of Sandy Hook victims.

II: Close to the Brokenhearted[‡]

The weapons and ammunition are all his.

The maids and hotel clerks, the loss of guests, of tourists, the glass, the gas in the cars, the ammunition of the cops, the cops, the EMTs and ambulances and gas in those buildings, the hospital and doctors and nurses, the coroner and morticians, the surgeons and undertakers, the casket makers, the lawyers and clerks and court fees, the calls home and to cell phones, the visits to houses in other parts of time, the witnessing of tears from people we do not know and cannot know

    —all that is ours.

....

[‡] Donald J. Trump quoting scripture after the Las Vegas Shooting.

PART IV

"We need the possibility of escape as surely as we need hope."

—Edward Albee

"If I'm free, it's because I'm always running."

—Jimi Hendrix, in an interview for
The Times, Sept. 5, 1970

"We gotta get out of this place."

—The Animals: Barry Mann,
Cynthia Weil.

Phoenix

she smashed a gnat—
or no-see-um—
beneath her thumb
against the wall.

it left a smudge
reminiscent of
an ash-made cross,
or a butterfly.

this delicate death
she wanted preserved
so took a kohl eye-lining
pencil and outlined

the shadowy new
animal that flew its
perpetual flight, knowing
that this too would smear,

would wipe away

would morph again

as she lived and as

she slept.

A Childhood

You can see light never stays still.
Light flickers
like my reflection on the Mississippi
when the water is too high
    (The sun is too high)
and we are too near it.

You keep testing the water
with a canvased-covered toe.
Mud thick along the crooked shore.
You keep sliding your hand into the water,
    wetting the edge of skin,
        shivering dramatically.

"It's so cold," you say.
It was, though the sun—
high enough that we can look up without seeing it
    bright enough to illuminate all,
    to see our reflections in the water
    colored by algae and plants and river fish—
warmed the air around us.

You and I watch ourselves move in the waters.
You and I: never still.

Funereal Ice Cream

It was almost too cold to listen or meet,
but in our wool suits and heavy dresses,
vanilla ice cream had never tasted so sweet.

We awaited the preacher to bleat
his sermon through breathy stresses.
It was almost too cold to listen or meet,

Still we sat through eulogist's praising treat,
the widow's sobbing, her child's messes.
Vanilla ice cream will never taste so sweet.

The children looked towards a later feat,
afraid for their own future egresses.
It was almost too cold to listen or meet.

The casket was removed from its seat,
by bearers who emerged from the recesses,
the thought of vanilla ice cream never so sweet.

And we congregated rose, hugged our fellow mourners,
promised to visit the gravesite in spring, but now
it was almost too cold to listen or pray.
Then, vanilla ice cream has never tasted so sweet.

Not Grass. Weeds.

Emily, stay in Amherst, watch the train
Weave through the brush of Fitchburg.

Fitzgerald, the American Dream doesn't involve
Dandelion yellow or sun-colored goatsbeard.

And Toni, even jazz—even the desired blue of
New England aster—won't suffice.

Maya, maybe the bird sings for untasted greens
Growing wantonly in our moneyed gardens.

And Phil, maybe this is the new pastoral:
Long green lawns without a speck of color.

Claudia, may the books brought to rallies
Be full of flowers and fruit mistaken for weeds.

Insects of France

The sun won't go down
It's late and hot
and Parisians don't seem to believe
in conditioned air.
Women go around with makeshift
paper fans, fanning their exposed throats
      << c'est chaud >>
         so hot

Parisians don't believe in window screens
Tonight, like last night:
a fly (une mouche)
A mosquito (un moustique)
un papillon noir all came inside
      (and a bird on my balcony
       balanced like birds do)
here bird: une mouche, un moustique
but leave me the black butterfly.

My American clothes are too
        conspicuous
And my well-oiled hair.
I dodge speaking and avoid scooters
I try not smiling when that is all
I've ever known
      all that was ever expected of me.

A green bug lands on my brown leg
I think in English
      (insect vert)
I let it crawl the width of my thigh
      (jambe brune)

I transpose:

[immigrant immigration
        migrant   migration
        refugee
                alien or expatriate   ]

Music notes from one voice
        to another

What is diaspora to this bug?
What do you call songs in unsingable keys?

Is home the same thing here?
I shoo the bug away
thinking how easily I place that word
on other places. Try to remember
where you come from. Try to know
where you're going.

II
Before I reached Paris,
three bites on the thick part of my thigh
and three more
        on my ankle.

There was much slapping and even a casualty
but who knows if it's the mosquito
who has my blood? Who knows
where she travels with ready proboscis?

And what has her grazing left behind?
An itch rife with disease.

It's silly, I know, still I imagine
my blood mingling with so many others—
a confused Parisian mosquito
nattering her way around
with a heavy diasporic blood
complicated by a love of country
that does not love her back.

Note to Self

If you fill another slot
Then you will be forced to stuff yourself,
        you will wrap yourself in others.

If the miller's daughter could have said no,
        admitted her inability to spin straw into gold—

        if you spun the wool you have,
        into the sweater you want
        knit and purl one loop with another wanted loop—

Then imagine the gold you'd have.

Intangible Love Story

Your hazy eyes roll
over me like fog
rolling over the bayou
or over the cityscape
during summer's brief dawn—

you: heavy as a hangover
groggy in the insufficient light
like seeing through mist mixed
with muck in a graveyard, you
cloud details and gloss words—

I try to see through your opaque airs,
fog lights glare through your miasmic
explanations, your demeanor, but
the bright sheen bounces
back, blinding me.

Wisdom of the Aesthetician

The aesthetician says that brows are back.
The aesthetician says that eyebrows help frame the face (or frames the face)
The aesthetician says full eyebrows are hip or hep (she has an accent)
The aesthetician says never to pluck, to always pluck, to come to her for plucking
The aesthetician has a mole that is almost inconspicuous, lingering over her eyebrow, and it's not quite round
The aesthetician says that some people just have beautiful eyes
    and I don't know if she's referring to the eye,
      the eyebrow, or
      the way the eyes set in the face
The aesthetician promises that the shape of my eyebrow informs my perspective on life
The aesthetician can't say "aesthetician" with an eyeliner pencil in her mouth—
    "aste-ca-ti-shih"
    —held like a cigarette, and I almost flinch from possible ash dumps
The aesthetician says she wants to see me back once a month
    But a month seems too long and I
    Worry my eyebrows will grow back
    What happens if a hair goes grey? Go stray?
    I want to see her more often;
    I want to see her every two weeks
    I want to try to discern the scent of her perfume every week
    I ask: would you live with me?
    And she doesn't hear me
      or pretends not to~

Confession

Your secrets run out before
you finish telling them, before
you finish finding people to tell,
before those you've told find others
to pass their secrets on and you see
them, your secrets, passing before
you, lapping you, making you tired
before the time has come for you
to make amends to the one person
you promised to not to tell confronts
you and looks at you—
and you look back,
and you can't help it—
you tell one more secret.

The one secret you didn't know you had.

They are here to assure you
it's not so bad, they are here
to pat your back: there, there,
they're here to make sure you'll
be fine, to whisper in your ear
as only friends can or as only
lovers can as only your sister
can your mother can,
they are here to hear your
confessions to them:

Tell them everything you couldn't utter.

The Squirrel Poem

Squirrel carcass on the side of MLK Drive
attracts curious crows and discarded cats
un-furloughed city worker with scraper and
water hose, swerving BMX bikes and
jaded pedestrians.

Squirrel running through the residential street
slowly. May have mange or something. Doesn't
look right. Keels over. A neighborhood dog works
herself off the leash, goes and licks the squirrel.

Squirrel's head in my side yard, jettisoned from neighbor's
window after they had their way with its body: skinned,
seasoned, roasted, served to a hungry family whose father
was used to Southern hunting, country meals.

The squirrel scrunched into a neighbor's squirrel trap,
an iron-maiden-esque spiral spilling down the pole
of his bird feeder. I looked into the squirrel's beady
eyes—a brown rich as Mideastern oil, sheen like
polished ebony. It chittered its squirrel talk at me,
wagged its wooly tail worriedly. I
avoided the claws—coarse as concrete—
and helped it go free.

Management of Lunatics,
with Illustrations of Insanity§

Lunatics need steering away from pretty things,
endearing things, such as blue butterflies that
batter outside of their compound. Mistakenly, I show
pictures of them to themselves, their skin slick in silver
nitrate and glossy paper, their eyes bulging or squinting or
staring defiantly up at the sun, sullen faces, sunken cheeks.
They stare and stare and stare at the pictures unsure
what is true and what is reality and whether those
two things are the same. "Here," one lunatic says,
her frame small, her voice large, her embodiment of life
as ripe as bananas browning in paper bags.
She takes the picture and draws succinct illustrations of
shadows on the surface of the photo. This is what they
were thinking when the picture was snapped.

Lunatics, maniacs, and women in general used to cross their
legs at the ankle for fear of eyes or spiders spying what
was hidden beneath skirts and flaps of flesh; they were careful
people and needed some management. "Here," said a
tall, thin willowy woman. She's a tree branch broken from a
slender tree, or a switch planted in the ground as if it should grow,
but stays still, sways, rots. "I will draw for you our concern," she says.
She wets a finger and traces the horrors in the sky, against the
forming clouds, I could plainly see that if I saw what she saw,
what any of them saw, I'd go mad. Considering

....

§ Title taking from a book by George Parkman, published in 1817
   https://archive.org/details/managementofluna00park

lunatics need some kind of direction—lunatics, maniacs, women—
they are all women, really, they are all big and little boned,
big and little hipped,
withering away into a world that would not have them
except to have them
and have a go, and they know this:
they show me how to walk on lotus feet,
how to breathe in corseted waists, how to endure the loss
of that location of sensual pleasure,
they show me scars and bruises perineal
lacerations and extended breasts, bleeding nipples and soreness—
so much soreness. I see them, finally, for what they are:
sane, so very sane.

Lady with Impunity

I watch a damselfly
dressed in iridescent colors
confusedly careen around a
green-colored pond full of tadpoles
in a verdant, New England woods.

I catch the glimpses of light
traveling through her wings
and follow her plunge through the
surface of the water;

she dips her pretty head in,
clearing her mind or her path.

Determined and certain,
she springs from the still waters,
causing a dollop of activity
spiraling in her wake.

I close my eyes and take
hold of a wing:
damselfly flies me away.

Age of Affirmation

When you're old enough to realize
that you can decide which of your parts are truly private,
it's too late for it to matter
or for you to care. The important thing

is apathy can be as delicious,
if not more so, than the bubble gum-flavored wishes
and over-caring of your past.
A friend asks *what part of your body*
do you appreciate more now that you're older

and you listen to answers other women give,
trying your best to come up with a reason,
trying to remember what part
you did like when you were not this age.

The lovely part here is outside of body,
within the mind, see:

thinking is grander now more than ever. You cherish
your every waking minute that you can turn over bits of
the world in your very own mind, you grasp at the
shimmering bits of dreams you barely remember,

falling vulnerably from dream to the shadows dancing
behind your closed lids—these visions are your most private
parts of you—and you fall, even more vulnerable
to being awake and aware.

Acknowledgments

Many of the poems in this collection have first appeared in the following magazines or anthologies:

Contrary Magazine, VerseWrights; Rag Queen Periodical; The Coil; Boston Accent Lit; Anomaly; Tishman Review; Former People: A Journal of Bangs and Whimpers; Eunoia Review; Progress and Tea; Nasty Women Poets: An Unapologetic Anthology of Subversive Verse, Blue Fifth Review; Elm Literary Magazine; From the Ashes: An International Anthology of Womxn's Poetry, Footnotes: A Literary Journal of History, No. 4; and *805 Lit + Art.* "Wisdom of the Aesthetician" was commissioned by artist Rachelle Beaudoin for a limited-edition art book on eyebrows.

Thank you to the following women for reading, listening, commenting, and encouraging: Rebecca L'Bahy, Laura Gail Grohe, Marci Haneisen, Eve Lyons (חוה ליונס), Rebecca Mills, Julie Rochlin, and Anastasia Vassos. Thank you to my fellow poets in one of the best workshop experiences ever, including Jonie McIntire, Adina Kopinsky, Amy Reichbach, Beth Spencer, Pam Rimington, Donna Weems, Evann Zuckerman, Sallie Hess, Ellie O'Leary, Mary Lucille DeBerry, and Leah Martin. Thanks to Julie Kane and Grace Bauer for directing some of my anger through a call for poems.

Thanks to Marge Piercy and the Marge Piercy Intensive Poetry Workshop for an involved week of poetry. Thanks to Leominster Public Library, for providing a space for Rebecca L'Bahy's poetry group. Thanks to Fitchburg State University for granting me time to write.

Finally, thanks to my loving family: my parents Maxine and Laurence and my sisters Rachelle, Prudence, and Natasha. Neal Delfeld, everything I do is because of you. Anaïs and Marlena, you couldn't be bothered, I know.

About the Author

DeMisty D. Bellinger has an MFA from Southampton College and a PhD from the University of Nebraska. She has published in many journals and anthologies, including *Contrary Magazine, Okay Donkey, The Rumpus, Necessary Fiction,* and *The Best Small Fictions: 2019.* She also has a poetry chapbook, *Rubbing Elbows* (Finishing Line Press). A Milwaukee native, DeMisty lives and teaches in central Massachusetts. You can find her website at demistybellinger.com.

More titles from Mason Jar Press

Call a Body Home
short stories chapbook by Michael Alessi

The Horror is Us
an anthology of horror fiction edited by Justin Sanders

Suppose Muscle Suppose Night Suppose This in August
memoir by Danielle Zaccagnino

Ashley Sugarnotch & the Wolf
poems by Elizabeth Deanna Morris Lakes

…and Other Disasters
short stories by Malka Older

The Couples
a novella by Nicole Callihan

All Friends Are Necessary
a novella by Tomas Moniz

Continental Breakfast
poetry by Danny Caine

How to Sit
memoir by Tyrese Coleman

Learn more at masonjarpress.com